Going Around The Corner

Taking the Gospel to Every Neighborhood in America

Leader Guide

Todd & Sheila Alewine
Around The Corner Ministries

aroundthecornerministries.org

Around The Corner Ministries exists to take the gospel to every neighborhood in America. Our mission is to equip followers of Jesus to engage their neighborhoods and communities with the gospel of Jesus Christ.

© 2017, 2020, 2024 by Todd & Sheila Alewine

ISBN 978-0-99913-182-4

All rights reserved. No part of this publication may be reproduced in any form without the written permission of *Around The Corner Ministries*, www.AroundTheCornerMinistries.org.

Scripture quotations taken from the New American Standard Bible® (NASB), Copyright © 1960, 1962, 1963, 1968, 1971, 1972, 1973, 1975, 1977, 1995 by The Lockman Foundation. Used by permission. www.Lockman.org.

Group Leader Guide

Dear Group Leader,

All over the world, God is calling unbelievers to Himself! And for some reason, He has chosen to use you and I to be a part of the great and holy work of spreading the gospel to all the world. Thank you for your commitment to be a disciple who makes disciples.

This leader guide is not meant to replace what God personally teaches you. We know that as you work through the Bible study ahead of your group, God will teach you about Himself, revealing truth and giving you insight into His Word. Treasure that process and know that God is speaking to you specifically so that you can lead and teach the people in your group. God knows what they need. We offer these discussion questions and ideas simply to prompt your thought process. It is a *guide*, not a lesson plan!

Here are a few tips for a successful group discussion.

1. **Do the work and expect the same of your members.** *Going Around The Corner* was intentionally written to focus on the scripture. All of us have opinions, ideas, and knowledge – but only the Word of God has the power to change a heart and redirect a life. The Word makes disciples.

2. **Give yourself time to meditate on the lessons.** Don't just answer the questions and move forward. Don't try to complete the entire lesson the night before – commit to daily study. Ponder the scriptures and allow God to speak to you. Keep a notebook nearby to write down your observations. As you share these thoughts with your group, you'll be amazed at how God has given you insight and wisdom that will speak personally and directly to each member.

3. **Cover the key truths.** Each week's study includes several scriptures, and it's easy to get lost in the discussion – God's Word is rich. To help you stay on track, the leader guide provides you with weekly "Key Truths." Make it a priority to cover these, as each lesson builds on the previous one.

4. **Select and answer discussion questions ahead of time.** We've given you "discussion starters" to guide your group. Be prepared by reading

through these ahead of time and think through how you would answer them. Then you'll be ready to prompt your members to take part in the group discussions.

5. **Encourage practical application.** This study is a simple, biblical, *practical* strategy for learning how to share the gospel and live on mission where God has placed you. Hold your members accountable for putting each week's concepts into practice. Go prayer walking with them. Practice sharing your stories with each other. We don't want to talk about "gospel theory" – we want to run the play.

6. **Pray first. Then pray.** We can't overemphasize the importance of prayer in this study. We have often defined it as a "prayer movement" as much as a training for sharing the gospel. God does the work ahead of us, in us, and through us. Without Him, we're just talking. So, pray. Pray often. Pray specifically and intentionally. Then watch God work!

As you lead your group through this discussion guide, here is a great way to remember each part of our strategy:

We are working in *His harvest*.
We are asking for *His heart*.
We are seeking *His glory*.
We are expecting *His salvation*.
We become *His disciples*.

The gospel is God's plan for the men and women He created, and we are simply offering ourselves as vessels for His Spirit to use. Keep these five words in mind each week, as you progress through the study, to help remind yourself and the members of your group of the real focus of this work: **Jesus** – it's all about **Him!**

Thank you for being used in God's kingdom work to teach and encourage believers. We're praying for you!

Todd & Sheila Alewine

How To Use This Study

*Go therefore and make disciples of all the nations, **baptizing [reaching]** them in the name of the Father and the Son and the Holy Spirit, **teaching** them to observe all that I commanded you; and lo, I am with you always, even to the end of the age.* (Matthew 28:19-20)

Going Around The Corner is a disciple-making study. We believe true discipleship is defined as "reaching" and "teaching," based on Jesus' words in Matthew 28. The first four chapters are focused on "reaching," while the last two chapters focus on "teaching." Both are important. If we are out of balance in one or the other, we are not making disciples.

We have found that the **first four chapters** can be taught effectively over six weeks.

Week 1 – Introduce study, distribute books, challenge members.
Week 2 – Session 1 (Exploring Your Neighborhood)
Week 3 – Session 2 (Engaging Your Neighbors Through Prayer)
Week 4 – Session 3 (Engaging Your Neighbors Through Good Works)
Week 5 – Session 4 (Evangelizing A Person Of Peace)
Week 6 – Review all material, challenge members to commit to implementing the study in their neighborhood, assign "Neighborhood Coaches."

The last chapter can be taught separately. Ideally, the members of your group will begin reaching out to their neighbors and co-workers using the strategy outlined in this study. As they develop relationships and begin sharing the gospel, you will want to come back together to hear their stories and encourage them. Coming back together for a week or two to finish the chapter on *Establishing New Believers In The Faith* would be a great second step.

In this way, you will truly be making disciples – by reaching and teaching!

Session 1
Exploring Your Neighborhood - His Harvest

> **KEY SCRIPTURE: Acts 17:24-26**
>
> *The God who made the world and all things in it, since He is Lord of heaven and earth, does not dwell in temples made with hands; nor is He served by human hands, as though He needed anything, since He Himself gives to all people life and breath and all things; and He made from one man every nation of mankind to live on all the face of the earth, having determined their appointed times and the boundaries of their habitation.*

Key Truths

1. The harvest belongs to God: it is *His harvest.*
2. God calls us to be "on mission" as His laborers.
3. God is sovereign over where we live, work and play.
4. Distractions and excuses are the enemy of the mission.
5. Prayer partners are key to the mission.

Discussion Questions

When you think of a missionary, what comes to mind?
Have you ever thought about where you live, work and play as your mission field?
What does it mean to be "sent"?
What did you learn about the harvest Jesus spoke about in Matthew 9:35-38?

Application Activity:
Have one or more individuals describe their "life journey," meaning the places they have lived and what circumstances caused them to move them each time. How did they get to where they live right now? Discuss how they see the sovereignty of God illustrated in their life, in getting them to this point in their journey.

BREAK-OUT OPTION: Divide a large group into smaller groups for this activity. When you come back together, ask someone to share what they learned about the sovereignty of God.

Ask:
What does it mean that God is "sovereign?" How important is it to you to believe this? How does this affect your life?

Discuss:
What part do *perspective* and *priorities* play in sharing our faith?
What is your greatest distraction when it comes to *living* your faith?
What distracts you from *sharing* your faith?

Ask:
What are some excuses we make to avoid doing something that we find challenging or difficult, such as sharing our faith? How can we overcome excuses?

Discuss:
What does it mean to not be "fit" for the kingdom of God? (Luke 9:62)
How do you "take up your cross" daily?

Ask:
Why do you think Jesus sent out the disciples in two's?
Does it scare you to be on mission where you live, work and play?

Action Step:
Have each person draw a rough diagram of their neighborhood, filling in names of the people they know. If they are focusing on a workplace or hobby, have them draw their office or place of work, or the place they spend time (gym, ball field, etc.), and label with the people they already know. Now have them indicate the people they see on a regular basis, or neighbors they haven't met yet. Challenge each person to commit to intentionally make an effort to get to know the spiritual condition of one or more of the people in their "mission field" by the next time you meet. Encourage them to bring the sheets back to group next week.

Close your session in prayer by breaking up into smaller groups and praying for the neighbors, co-workers or friends on your sheets by name.

Session 2
Engaging Neighbors Through Prayer: His Heart

> **KEY SCRIPTURE: Matthew 9:35-38**
>
> *Jesus was going through all the cities and villages, teaching in their synagogues and proclaiming the gospel of the kingdom, and healing every kind of disease and every kind of sickness. Seeing the people, He felt compassion for them, because they were distressed and dispirited like sheep without a shepherd. Then He said to His disciples, "The harvest is plentiful, but the workers are few. Therefore, beseech the Lord of the harvest to send out workers into His harvest."*

Key Truths

1. Prayer isn't something we do before the mission; prayer is the mission.
2. Praying to the Lord of the harvest gives us *His heart* for the lost.
3. Listening is as important as praying/asking: learning to be Spirit-led.
4. Prayer walking gives insight while we are "on-site."
5. God has people of peace for us to meet.

Review From Last Week:
Ask the group to share if they were able to meet any new people where they live, work and play. Was anyone able to engage someone in a spiritual conversation, or share the gospel? Ask if anyone can share where they saw the sovereignty of God at work.

Discussion Questions

What does the word engage mean?
What is the purpose of engaging our neighbors?

Discuss:
What do you learn about prayer from Acts 2:1-11? Why did the disciples not immediately act on Jesus' instructions? Describe a time when God told you to wait. Were you obedient? What was the result?

Discuss:
Read Acts 2:5 to the group. Why is this significant?

Ask:
What does it mean to prayer walk? Have you ever gone on a prayer walk? Share about this experience with the group.

Ask:
What does it mean to "pray on site with insight"?
How does prayer walking help you know how to pray for your neighbors?

Discuss:
What does it mean to listen to the prompts of the Spirit? Has the Spirit ever prompted you to do something? How did you know it was God that was speaking? What was the result?

Review the story in Acts 8:25-40. What practical applications did you find for your own life in the story of Philip and the Ethiopian man?

Discuss:
Have you thought about a person of peace, as described in Luke 10:5?
Do you know of a time that the Lord led you to a person of peace? What was the outcome? Have you ever felt when talking with someone who was not open to the gospel that it was time to "shake the dust off your feet"?

Ask:
What did Peter learn about being open to sharing the gospel with all people (Acts 10)? Are there any people or groups of people with whom you would be uncomfortable sharing the gospel? Why? What do you think God would say?

Action Step:
Have each person review their drawing of their neighborhood or workplace and indicate to the best of their knowledge if they believe each person/house could be a "person of peace" (open to hearing the gospel) or if they are already a believer. Start praying specifically for them, by name.

Close in prayer, asking God to give each person boldness to begin praying regularly and specifically over their neighbors – the people with whom they live, work and play.

Session 3
Engaging Neighbors Through Good Works: His Glory

> **KEY SCRIPTURE: Matthew 5:16**
>
> *Let your light shine before men in such a way that they may see your good works, and glorify your Father who is in heaven.*

Key Truths

1. We must love God before we can love our neighbor.
2. Our neighbor is "anyone who is in front of us."
3. God orchestrates our steps for sovereign, divine appointments.
4. Being a good neighbor involves compassion, care and commitment.
5. Good works are only good when they bring glory to God.

Review From Last Week:
Ask the group if anyone was able to meet a fellow believer and invite them to join in praying for their neighbors. Did anyone go on a prayer walk? Did they *happen* to meet anyone? Was anyone able to share the gospel or engage in a spiritual conversation?

Discussion Questions

Ask:
What is a very important prerequisite of loving our neighbors?

Discuss:
What does it mean to love God?
How do we love God practically, with our heart, soul, mind and strength?
Why is loving God important to loving and serving our neighbors?

Ask:
What did Jesus say proves that someone is a good neighbor?
What does mercy look like in everyday life?

Application Activity:
Have the group brainstorm a modern-day example of the story of the Good Samaritan. Define a physical or felt need you have observed. Who would be the person in need? The priest? The Levite? The Samaritan? The innkeeper? Require their story to be relevant for today.

BREAK-OUT OPTION: Break into small groups and have each group present a short skit.

Discuss:
How can we imitate the Good Samaritan's response to a person in need? According to what you studied on Day 3 and Day 4, what attitudes or actions are necessary to be a good neighbor? Are these attitudes or actions applicable and relevant to the people who live next door, or the person who works beside you? How?

Ask:
Which person best characterizes your relationships with your neighbors and co-workers: the priest, the Levite, or the Samaritan?
What comforts would you have to give up to live on mission in your neighborhood?

Discuss:
What are good works? What is the purpose of good works?
How do good works bring glory to God?

<u>**Action Step**</u>:
Ask each member of the group to consider this question: *Who has God placed on your heart, that you know He is calling you to reach out to?* When they have someone in mind, have them write down at least three ways they could engage this person, through a good deed, or showing mercy. Encourage them to think of something that is very practical. Then challenge them to act on this idea this week.

Close your session by breaking up in groups of two or three to brainstorm practical ways of reaching specific neighbors, then praying for one another to act, and for the neighbors to see the love of Christ in those actions.

Session 4
Evangelizing a Person of Peace: His Salvation

> **KEY SCRIPTURE: Luke 2:25-32**
>
> *And there was a man in Jerusalem whose name was Simeon; and this man was righteous and devout, looking for the consolation of Israel; and the Holy Spirit was upon him. And it had been revealed to him by the Holy Spirit that he would not see death before he had seen the Lord's Christ. And he came in the Spirit into the temple; and when the parents brought in the child Jesus, to carry out for Him the custom of the Law, then he took Him into his arms, and blessed God, and said, "Now Lord, You are releasing Your bond-servant to depart in peace, according to Your word; For my eyes have seen **Your salvation**, which You have prepared in the presence of all peoples, A LIGHT OF REVELATION TO THE GENTILES, and the glory of Your people Israel."*

Key Truths

1. As believers, we are all commanded to share the gospel.
2. Jesus is the only way to salvation; people will perish apart from Christ.
3. As believers, we all have a story to tell.
4. We must share the complete gospel: creation, fall, redemption, restoration.
5. Sharing the gospel begins with intentional, purposeful conversations.

***Review From Last Week*:**
Ask for individuals to share if they were able to engage someone through good deeds over the last week. What was the response?

Discussion Questions

***Ask*:**
What keeps people from sharing their faith?
What keeps *you* from sharing *your* story?

Ask:
Who led you to faith in Jesus Christ?
Have you led anyone to faith in Jesus Christ?

Discuss:
Print out the following scriptures on individual slips of paper and pass them out. Have them read aloud, and ask the question: *What does this verse tell me I must believe in order to share the gospel?*
Romans 1:14-17, Acts 4:12, Acts 4:20, 2 Corinthians 5:14-15, 2 Corinthians 5:20, John 3:16

BREAK-OUT OPTION: Break into small groups for this activity.

Discuss:
Discuss the Gospel as summed up in four words: **Creation**, **Fall**, **Redemption** and **Restoration**. Why is it important to be able to share each part of the complete gospel? How does this help explain the gospel to someone who may never have heard it, or who has only heard parts of it?

<u>Group Activity</u>:
Ask for a volunteer to retell Zaccheus' story from Luke 19:1-10, using the four questions below as a guide. If no one volunteers, be prepared to tell it yourself! Discuss Zaccheus' conversion, reminding the group that the real miracle was not that he saw Jesus, but that *Jesus saw Zaccheus!*
1. What was Zaccheus' life before meeting Jesus?
2. How did Zaccheus demonstrate his need for Jesus?
3. How did Zaccheus become a Christ-follower/believer?
4. What changed in Zaccheus' life?

Now have someone volunteer to tell their own story, using the same four questions. Tell your own story as an example, if the group is hesitant to participate. Discuss how they can share their own story of meeting Jesus in just five minutes.

Ask:
How do you turn a conversation to Christ?
What keeps people from discussing spiritual things? Do you think people are afraid to talk about spiritual things, or to talk about Jesus?

Practical Lesson: TURNING CONVERSATIONS TOWARD CHRIST

Use the information below to teach the members of your group how to turn conversations. If possible, plan ahead with several individuals to role play as an example.

First, **explore**...opening doors to discover as much as you can about the person. We do this by using two kinds of questions, which build on each other.

Surface Questions:
- Where did you grow up?
- What sports do you like?
- What are your hobbies?

Personal Questions:
- Are you married? Do you have children?
- Do you have pets?
- What do you do for a living?
- What are places you have traveled or lived?
- What did you enjoy there?

Second, **engage**...turn your conversation in the direction of the gospel. Use the third type of question to find out the spiritual interest, and as a bridge toward deeper questions. Think of this as a "pivot" question.

Religious Questions:
- What did you do on the weekends growing up?
- Did you attend church as a child?
- Did you get married at a church?
- Did you come from a religious family?

Finally, **evangelize**...if the person is open and truly seeking the Lord (a *person of peace*), move toward the fourth type of question.

Spiritual Questions:
- What do you think about Jesus?
- Are you a Christian?
- Do you have a personal relationship with Jesus?
- Can I tell you my story of how I met Jesus?

If a person is willing to hear your story, be sure to integrate the complete gospel as you share.

Action Step:

Challenge each person to practice telling their own story to others during the week, and to pray for opportunities to share it with an unbeliever. Ask if anyone has a person in mind they know God is calling them to share the gospel with. Pray for that person.

Close your session in prayer by asking God to give each person an opportunity to share their story, and for boldness in sharing their faith.

Session 5
Establishing New Believers in the Faith: His Disciples

> **KEY SCRIPTURE: Colossians 2:6-7**
>
> *Therefore as you have received Christ Jesus the Lord, so walk in Him, having been firmly rooted and now being built up in Him and established in your faith, just as you were instructed, and overflowing with gratitude.*

Key Truths

1. Leading a person to Christ brings a responsibility to help them grow in their faith and establish them in spiritual truths.
2. Personal discipleship requires commitment of our time, energy and resources to another believer.
3. New believers need assurance of salvation, and an understanding of God, the Bible, the Holy Spirit, and prayer.
4. New believers must learn to worship.

Review From Last Week:
Ask if anyone was able to share their story this week. If so, let them describe what happened, how they felt, and what they learned from the experience.

Discussion Questions

What does it mean to be "established" in the faith?
What does it mean to "walk" in Christ? (Colossians 2:6-7)
Why is important to be "rooted" and "built up"?

Discuss:
When you became a believer, were you discipled or mentored? If so, how did this help you get started in your new relationship with Christ? If you were not discipled, how did that affect your growth as a new believer? What are some things you wished you would have known about being a Christian as you look back?

Ask:
Have you ever discipled anyone?
What was your experience?

Discuss:
Review the examples of disciple-makers you studied on Day 2. What did you learn from each of the examples? How does this help you as you think about discipling a young believer?

Ask:
What is the end goal of discipleship?
What did Jesus mean when He instructed the disciples to *teach* in Matthew 28:19-20?
What did you learn from Paul's relationship with the believers? (Day 3)

Group Activity:
Break out into small groups. Instruct the members to refer to Day 4 in their Bible study. As time permits, discuss each area in which a new believer must be established. Why is each one important? Where do you feel you may be lacking personally?

Ask:
How do you define community?
What does "community" look like biblically and practically?

Discuss:
Do you agree with what John Piper said about worship and missions? How does missions lead to worship? How does worship lead to missions?

<u>**Action Step**</u>:
Challenge each member of your group to consider where they are in the cycle of discipleship. Ask the group how they will implement what they have learned into their daily life. Ask them to share one practical way they will adjust their life in response to the mission of sharing Christ. Encourage them to continue their commitment to being used by God in His harvest that is right around them.

As a group, pray for one another as you go out into the mission field where God has placed each one of you.

NOW WHAT?

Suggestions For Implementation

Congratulations. You've completed this Bible study! But now what?

Instead of the last lesson being the end, let it be the beginning! We're praying that God has stirred the hearts of your group with a passion to reach their neighborhoods and workplaces with the gospel. Hopefully they are already implementing this strategy right where they live, work and play, and that you are already seeing kingdom growth that is impacting your church. Here are a few suggestions to help them continue to run the play.

Be strategic. Where do your people live? Get out a map and mark the neighborhoods. Assign "neighborhood coaches" to encourage ownership. Let them really see the harvest where God has sovereignly planted them.

Be accountable. Accountability = Encouragement. Don't let the excitement dwindle. Plan a time now to meet again and share stories, successes, failures, fears, and victories. Ask the hard questions: Who are you praying for? Who have you shared with?

Be praying. Encourage your people not only to pray for the salvation of the people in their neighborhoods, but also to "pray for laborers for the harvest." Hold prayer meetings in your homes, with other believers in your neighborhood.

Be bold. It is very easy to focus on praying and good works, and never share the gospel. Encourage one another to speak the gospel, as well as demonstrate it. The only way to become more comfortable in sharing the gospel is to do it – again and again!

Be intentional. As your people begin to make disciples, be sure to provide them with the resources to help new believers grow in their faith and become part of the local church body. Then they too, will go out and make disciples.

We would love to hear how this study has impacted you and your group. Email us at todd@aroundthecornerministries.org.

ATCM Resources

aroundthecornerministries.org

Be Strategic With The Gospel

Going Around The Corner Bible Study
ISBN: 9780692781999 / List Price: $12.99
This six-session workbook helps believers explore the mission field in their own neighborhoods and workplaces. Learn to engage others through prayer and biblical good works guided by the prompts of the Holy Spirit. Gain confidence to evangelize through sharing the complete gospel and your own story. Discover how to establish and equip new believers in their faith journey. A simple, practical and biblical strategy for disciple-making.

Going Around The Corner Bible Study, Student Edition
ISBN: 9780999131831 / List Price: $10.99
This five-session workbook helps high school and college students explore the mission field of campus, team, neighborhood and workplace. Students will begin to see their friends and teammates through the eyes of the gospel and be equipped to share their faith.

Going Around The Corner Bible Study, Leader Guide
ISBN: 9780999131824 / List Price: $3.99
Key truths for each week, helpful discussion starters and thoughtful questions to help your group apply the principles in the study, plus suggested group activities and practical application steps. Adaptable for use with the Student Edition.

Be Aware Of The Gospel

40 Days of Spiritual Awareness
ISBN: 9780999131800 / List Price: $9.99
A devotional to understand who God is and how He is working in the people right around you. Discover truth that will increase your awareness of God, yourself, other believers, and unbelievers. Be reminded of what is important: an awareness of God's work in our world, as He redeems and saves. At the end of the journey, you will realize that you are an important part of accomplishing that work and be prepared to join Him.

Be Refreshed In The Gospel

Grace & Glory: A 50-Day Journey In The Purpose & Plan Of God
ISBN: 9780999131848 / List Price $11.99

What do we do when we face a crisis of faith? When everything we believe is challenged? That's when we must discover (or re-discover) God's purpose for our lives and learn to live with a mindset of His grace...grace that reveals His glory. This devotional will refresh believers in the gospel and encourage them to live every day so that the glory of God will be proclaimed by the power of grace at work in their lives.

Pray The Gospel
Just Pray: God's Not Done With You
ISBN: 9780999131886 / List Price $9.99

If you ever think, "What good am I to the kingdom anymore?" this devotional is for you. You are strategically, sovereignly positioned to have kingdom impact in this generation through a simple commitment to prayer. God is not looking for people of strength and confidence. He is seeking those who know they are helpless and weak so that His strength and glory can be made magnified in them. No matter what your challenges or limitations are, God still has work for you to do for the kingdom. We invite you to accept the challenge and just pray.

Run With The Gospel
Let Us Run The Race
ISBN: 9781733047807 / List Price $9.99

Wisdom and insight from Paul's letter to the church at Philippi. Called the greatest missionary of all time, Paul made an unforgettable and enduring impact on the world and the culture that surrounded him. If we could sit down and chat with him, what would he tell us? What can we learn from a man who ran his race so well? All of us desire to make our lives count for something greater than ourselves. The reality is, there is no greater call than the cause of Christ and the gospel of His kingdom. Let's pursue Him with passion, endurance and joy. Let's run the race, for Jesus is worthy.

Give The Gift Of The Gospel
Living In Light of the Manger
ISBN: 9780999131817 / List Price $9.99

If the manger only has meaning during our holiday celebrations, we've missed the point of the story. Jesus was born, so that we could be *born again*. The events of His birth and the people who welcomed Him have many lessons to teach us about the glorious gospel and how Jesus came to change our lives. Discover the purpose and power of the manger. Perfect as a gift to introduce the gospel to friends, co-workers and neighbors.

Check out our website bookstore for additional resources!

www.ingramcontent.com/pod-product-compliance
Lightning Source LLC
Chambersburg PA
CBHW050451010526
44118CB00013B/1783